Adelaide AND
Agriculture

May your harvest always
be plentiful! ♡ Roslyn

♡ Suzette Juliette ♡

Written by Roslyn Haynie Banks,
Suzette Banks, and Juliette Banks
Illustrated by Bonnie Lemaire

ISBN: 978-1-7361942-4-9 Paperback

ISBN: 978-1-7361942-3-2 Hardcover
Library of Congress Control Number: 2023910742

Written by Roslyn Haynie Banks with Suzette Banks and Juliette Banks
Edited by Candice L. Davis
Illustrations and cover by Bonnie Lemaire
Published by Adelaide Farms, LLC in Lottsburg, Virginia

This book provides a general overview of a week in the life of African American, female, family farmers in the rural Northern Neck of Virginia. The authors explore agricultural career options as they relate to science, technology, engineering, arts, and math (STEAM). Using a liberal arts and STEAM educational foundation, these leaders overcome traditional barriers and obstacles that previously stunted economic growth for small family-farming operations. This book is the authors' personal tribute to the Haynie family-farming legacy and represents our vision for future sustainable family farms globally.

Cataloging-in-Publication Data has been applied for and may be obtained from the Library of Congress.

We dedicate this book to children, community helpers, and agricultural workers all over the world. It is never too early to gain an appreciation of agriculture and entrepreneurship.

We pay homage to our ancestors and the original inhabitants of this country who cultivated the land in unpleasant conditions. We thank those who have utilized technology to improve life on the family farm for safer and more efficient operations.

We thank God for allowing our family to sustain six generations of land ownership and farming to feed and clothe the world.

-Suzette Banks & Juliette Banks

To my daughters, may you always cherish your childhood and appreciate your heritage. Remember your family values, trust your training, and follow your instincts.

I would like to publicly acknowledge and thank our village of family, friends, church members, sorority sisters, educators, mentors, clients, colleagues, and community helpers who have helped me and my family become better global citizens.

To our readers, thank you for purchasing an authentic copy of this publication to sow seeds into the next generation of world leaders. Wealth includes tangible and intangible assets like money, property, family values, work ethics, and a good reputation.

-Roslyn Haynie Banks

This book was given to:

_____

From:

_____

Occasion or message:

On an old plantation in Virginia
near the Chesapeake Bay,
lived two girls who dreamt
of what they would become one day.

Row crop farmers produce commodities,
including corn and soybeans.
The girls expand the Haynie farming operations
and include microgreens.

"What are farmers?
What do they do?"

Let's follow Adelaide.
She will guide you.

CHESAPEAKE
Bay

On Monday, we take invoices to the factory.

In the water, we spy an osprey nest.

Truck drivers prepare for a special delivery.

The Coast Guard keeps the Bay looking it's best.

The Chesapeake Bay is an estuary,

where fresh and saltwater meet.

Marine scientists study the biology

of blue crabs we love to eat.

Down at the dock of the bay,

we check our crab pots and oyster floats.

Later, we watch the sunset tides roll away,

and read stories about mermaids and boats.

On Tuesday, Bonnie the botanist teaches us
about growing peanuts, cotton, and rice.
We meet with vendors to discuss
technology to profit in snow and in ice.

Our ancestors farmed with simple hand tools,

as a family we pray and work together as a team.

Our wish is forty acres and two mules,

with faith we can accomplish our dream.

Farming is not just about plows and cows anymore,

we share new developments with the crew.

Today's farmers use technology and gadgets galore,

GPS technology and aerial drones provide an eagle's view.

On Wednesday, we visit storm damage projects.

We hire an arborist to inspect the bad parts.

Elizabeth the engineer creates new objects.

Respect for nature runs deep in our hearts.

Erosion is another hazard in our waterfront town.

We are thankful for generators and solar technology!

Power stops when overhead lines are knocked down.

Electrical engineers respond quickly to restore energy.

Suzette operates the excavator to clean up the limbs.

To replace what was lost, we plant a mustard seed tree.

Juliette and I sort the recycling bins.

Our legacy includes faith, family, and farming.

We must have all three!

On Thursday, we prepare lavender for an event.

April showers bring May flowers, so we monitor the rain.

Agritourism connects people to farms as we celebrate in a tent.

Silly boys, girls can farm too. Don't tell us to "stay in our lane."

At the produce stand, we build with recycled wood.

With fresh compost and soil, we dig holes to plant.

Our rose garden makes the fresh air smell good.

For help with social media, we call on their aunt.

Suzette and Juliette want a petting zoo.

I planted a vineyard and learned to make wine.

Virginia the veterinarian brings pigs, sheep, and ducks too!

The whole town is excited. This vision is truly divine.

On Friday, I calculate payroll taxes and wages.

I manage resources wisely. Money does not grow on a tree.

As chief financial officer, my job is to expand revenue in phases.

In farming remember that patience is key.

The notary public stamps a deed with her seal.

There are 43,560 square feet in a one-acre plot.

Accountants determine capital gains on a real estate deal.

Math skills help me calculate amounts on the spot.

We remember Jesus died for our sin.

We celebrate the seven last words as a community.

The Bible says believers shall also win!

Jesus paid the price of sin for you and for me!

Saturday, we visit Jamestown for history lessons.

By God's grace and mercy, we have overcome a lot.

Our ancestors worked, sang, and prayed for blessings.

I meet with friends from college at my sorority plot.

Easter Sunday, we attend sunrise service on the beach.

Jesus was raised from the dead,

nothing separates us from His reach.

Back on the farm, we prepare a soulful dinner for the entire family.

Before breaking bread, we thank God for the land, laborers, and our legacy!

By the end of the week, the girls know what they want to be.

At the same time, they rejoice and say, "Entrepreneurship is for me!"

Dear readers,

Thank you for supporting our small business by reading and sharing the information in this book! We attempted to explain a week in the life on the Haynie family farm. We tried to connect students with community helper roles they have already explored and introduce new career possibilities.

We were born into an entrepreneurial family. An entrepreneur is someone who solves problems and operates a business with the goal of making a profit by providing products and services to customers. When Roslyn was in high school, our family owned and operated over seven separate businesses. After high school, Roslyn left the family farm to study business and international finance. After working for large corporations for over a decade, she returned to the family farm to give her daughters an entrepreneurial foundation like the one she received in her hometown.

We hope this book sows an early appreciation for agriculture in our readers from urban, suburban, and rural communities alike! It is designed for readers of all ages, to be read repeatedly as you grow and become more advanced with the role of agricultural workers and agricultural economics.

This book is ideal for bulk graduation gifts, afterschool or summer programs, and back-to-school supply drives. Please contact the author directly for bulk purchase discounts and tax-exempt organization sales.

Glossary

ACCOUNTANT – a person who maintains and interprets financial records. Accountants can work in public accounting firms, governments, not–for–profit organizations, publicly traded companies, or privately–owned businesses.

ACCOUNTING – a process of systematically recording, managing, and presenting financial accounts and transactions. The rules–based system of accounting allows users to monitor and compare financial data including revenue, expenses, and capital. Accounting is also commonly referred to as "the language of business".

ACRE – a unit of area used to measure fields, pastures, and other land. One acre is 4,840 square yards or 43,560 square feet (almost the size of a football field).

AGRICULTURE – everything involved in using land for growing and harvesting plants, and raising animals to be used for food, fiber, fabrics, and fuel. It includes the production, processing, and transportation of farm products, research to improve plant and animal genetics, and other things farmers use.

AGRITOURISM – touring agriculture areas including farms and vineyards for knowledge and recreation. (Agriculture + Tourism = Agritourism). Popular examples that we enjoy include pumpkin patches, Christmas tree farms, corn mazes, petting zoos, and strawberry picking patches.

ANCESTOR – a person from whom one descended. Also commonly known as a forefather.

ANGEL INVESTOR – a private investor who provides money for small startups or entrepreneurs.

AQUACULTURE – growing animals and cultivating plants that live in water, like fish, shellfish, and algae for food.

ARBORIST – a person who maintains and cares for trees and shrubs. He or she also identifies disease and insect problems and uses appropriate treatments.

ASSET – a valuable resource that can generate cash flow, reduce expenses, pay debt, or improve sales.

BIOLOGY – the study of living things. Botany, ecology, and zoology are all branches of biology.

BOTANIST – a person skilled in biology, the science of plants, and plant life.

BUSHEL – a unit of volume used to measure grain or blue crabs by weight. Equal to about eight US dry gallons. A standard weight is assigned to each commodity measured in bushels. One bushel of wheat at 13.5% moisture is approximately 60 pounds.

CAPITAL GAINS – the profit from the sale of an asset that has increased in value over time.

CERTIFIED PUBLIC ACCOUNTANT (CPA) – a person who has met all statutory and licensing requirements in the state where he or she works. The CPA designation helps regulate professional standards in the accounting industry. CPAs can provide auditing, bookkeeping, forensic accounting, and managerial accounting services.

CHEMISTRY – the study of substances and their properties and how they react with each other.

CHESAPEAKE BAY – the largest estuary in the United States measuring almost 200 miles long and up to 30 miles at its widest point. Located between Maryland and Virginia, this body of water is essential to the economy of both states and provides many different career opportunities. It is nicknamed "the great shellfish bay" for the popular blue crabs, oysters, and rockfish.

CHIEF FINANCIAL OFFICER – a person primarily responsible for managing all financial aspects of a company or organization. Duties include financial planning, managing risks, keeping accurate books and reporting records, and analyzing financial data.

COMMODITY – a product or service that is indistinguishable between competitors. Common examples include raw materials such as corn, wheat, sugar, coffee, copper, natural gas, and building supplies.

COMPOST – a mixture of dying organic substances, such as plant material, vegetable peels, and manure, used to fertilize soil.

DEADLINE – a date or time before which something must be done.

DEED – a written and signed instrument used to legally convey or transfer ownership of property.

DEPRECIATION – an accounting concept that measures the decrease in value of an asset over time as it is used in a trade or business due to normal wear and tear.

DIVINE – of, related to, or coming directly from God or a deity.

DRONE – an unmanned aerial vehicle (UAV), guided remotely to take aerial pictures or measurements of land to monitor crop production, soil variations, and irrigation levels. These devices can also be used to apply water, fertilizers, pesticides, or other chemicals to growing crops. Agricultural drones provide data to help farmers make better decisions or to solve specific problems with crops or livestock.

ECOLOGY– a department within biology that studies how living things interact with their environment and with each other.

ECONOMICS – the social science of production, distribution, and consumption of goods and services of a society, most commonly expressed in financial terms.

ECONOMY – the resources and wealth of a community, typically measured in terms of production and consumption of goods and services.

ENGINEER – a person skilled in designing, building, and maintaining engines, machines, and structures. There are many specialties under this discipline such as aerospace, agricultural, chemical, civil, electrical, environmental, and mechanical.

ENROLLED AGENT (EA) – a person who has earned the privilege of representing taxpayers before the Internal Revenue Service. Enrolled agent status is the highest credential awarded by the IRS. Enrolled Agents must adhere to ethical standards and complete numerous hours of continuing education courses annually.

ENTREPRENEUR – a person who organizes and operates a business with the goal of making a profit by providing products and services to customers.

ENVIRONMENT – a place or surroundings of something. Includes living and non–living things.

EROSION – the gradual washing and wearing away of the earth's surface by wind, water, or other elements.

ESTUARY – a place where a large river meets the sea and fresh water and saltwater mix together (brackish water). The Chesapeake Bay is the largest estuary in the United States and is an extremely productive natural habitat because of the high level of nutrients.

EXCAVATOR – a machine that lifts up or removes soil and other materials from the ground.

FINANCE – the study of money, investments, and other financial instruments with the intent to analyze and interpret accounting information to make business decisions.

FINANCIAL LITERACY – skills and knowledge necessary to understand how money works. Includes concepts of money management, budgeting, saving, investing, lending, and borrowing. Roslyn's goal is that readers will make age–appropriate informed decisions and foster a sense of personal financial well–being.

GENERATOR – a machine that converts mechanical energy into electricity. Sources of energy can include steam, gas, water, internal combustion, wind, or a hand crank.

GENETIC ENGINEERING – plant breeding or modification of characteristics by manipulating genetic material to create sought-after effects in growing plants or animals.

GEOLOGY – the study of the Earth's structure (including rocks) on and under the surface.

GPS – Global Positioning System (GPS) is a satellite-based radio navigation system that constantly sends signals to the earth to provide location tracking and positioning capabilities.

HABITAT – a home or natural environment of a person, animal, plant, or other organism.

INTERCROPPING – growing different kinds of plants together so that each benefit from the other. Examples include cotton and peanuts, or tomatoes and marigolds.

INVESTOR – a person or organization who puts money at risk with the goal of making a profit.

INVOICE – a list of goods sent or services provided with a statement requesting payment.

JAMESTOWN – the first permanent English settlement in the Americas, established in 1607. Located in Virginia on the James River.

LAVENDER – a purple colored flowering plant used for many purposes including decoration, cooking, medicine, creating skin care products, or extracting essential oils.

LIVESTOCK – animals raised for use and profit in farming. Includes cattle, horses, pigs, poultry, sheep, and similar animals.

MACHETE – a large, heavy knife used as a tool to harvest crops or to clear small trees and shrubs.

MENHADEN – a large fish that produces valuable oil used to make fish meal, fertilizer, and medical supplements. Menhaden are part of the herring family and primarily live on the east coast of North America.

MICROGREENS – the young shoots of salad vegetables that are harvested for consumption just after the first leaves have developed. Examples include lettuce, mint, radish, and spinach.

MONEY – legal tender to exchange goods and services. Money includes negotiable instruments such as currency, coins, and checks.

NOTARY PUBLIC – a person authorized to perform certain legal transactions and to impartially witness signatures on important business documents and deeds.

OSPREY – a large bird of prey that arrives to the Chesapeake Bay in spring from South America. Osprey eat fish and have long, narrow wings with a white underside. Also called a "fish hawk".

PAYROLL TAXES – taxes assessed on the wages, tips, and salaries of employees. The four major types of payroll taxes are income taxes, unemployment insurance, Social Security taxes, and Medicare taxes.

PLANTATION – a large-scale estate or farming operation know for growing profitable crops. Typically contains a private residence or home on the property. Also referred to as a ranch, orchard, hacienda, vineyard, or homestead.

PLOW – a farming tool with blades to break up the soil and turn it over to prepare for planting seeds.

POLLEN – a yellow sticky powder made from flowering plants to fertilize. Sometimes causes allergic reactions or allergy to humans when it is in the air.

POLLINATION – moving pollen from one flower to another. This is usually done by animals (pollinators) such as birds, bees, and butterflies and it helps seeds to grow.

POLLUTANTS – substances that have harmful impacts to the environment.

PRODUCE – farm-produced crops. Usually refers to fresh, unprocessed, fruits and vegetables.

PROFIT – the mathematical difference between income and expenses of a trade or business.

REVENUE – total income or cash receipts produced by a given source.

SOIL – the layer of dirt and earth where plants grow.

SOLAR – of, relating to, or using the energy of the sun. The Sun is the most important source of energy to support the life of people and plants on Earth.

SORORITY – an organization for women to come together for common social or community service purposes.

STEAM – acronym for Science, Technology, Engineering, Arts, and Math disciplines.

SUSTAINABLE – able to be maintained or upheld at a certain level or rate. An activity that permanently damages an environment or use up (depletes) things needed for the population to survive is not sustainable.

TAX – a fee levied on individuals, corporations, trusts, or estates to pay for government services. Common examples include public works, roads, infrastructure, military protection, schools, and parks.

TECHNOLOGY – the application of knowledge to achieve everyday goals in a reproducible way. Technology has enhanced our farm operations by combining innovation and software to equipment, machines, and tools.

TIDES – the rise and fall of ocean levels caused by the gravitational forces of the moon, sun, and Earth orbiting one another. Commonly referred to as "high tide" or "low tide".

TOXIC – poisonous or extremely harmful.

VENDOR – a person or business that sells a product or service. Also known as a seller, dealer, merchant, or merchandiser.

VETERINARIAN – a person skillfully trained in the science of caring for injuries and illnesses of animals.

VINEYARD – an area where grapevines are planted, primarily for winemaking.

WAGES – money paid by an employer to an employee for their labor or services.

WEALTH – the value of all assets (tangible and intangible) possessed by a person, family, organization, or country.

Extend the Lesson Activity

Use this space to think about community helpers who work in the science, technology, engineering, arts, and math (STEAM) fields. In this book, we explore careers in our small-town rural community. Write your thoughts about each character in the space provided.

How do they impact the food you eat? How do they interact with the Chesapeake Bay and the environment? Who in your community works in similar roles? Interview them and ask how and why they chose that career path.

Adelaide the Accountant

_____

_____

_____

_____

_____

_____

Bonnie the Botanist

_____
_____
_____
_____

Virginia the Veterinarian

_____
_____
_____
_____

Allison the Arborist

_____
_____
_____
_____

Elizabeth the Engineer

_____
_____
_____
_____

Roslyn's Chicken Pot Pie Recipe

* Children, always ask an adult for assistance and supervision when cooking.

Ingredients:

2 refrigerated pie crusts (or one rolled and one pie crust in a pan) at room temperature

1-pound boneless skinless chicken breasts

1/2 teaspoon Lawry's seasoning salt

1/2 teaspoon black pepper

2 tablespoons butter, divided

16 oz frozen mixed vegetables (peas, carrots, green beans, etc.) thawed and drained

1/2 can diced potatoes (drained)

2 cans condensed cream of chicken soup 10.5oz (can substitute cream of mushroom if desired)

1/3 cup of white milk

Directions:

1. Preheat oven to 425° Fahrenheit. Add a little oil or butter to the bottom of the pan to prevent sticking. Bake bottom pie crust in a deep round baking glass dish for 5-8 minutes for a flaky bottom layer and remove from oven.

2. Thinly dice chicken breast into chunks and cook in a skillet over medium-high heat. Season chicken to your taste preferences with seasoning salt, black pepper, and one tablespoon of butter.

3. Reduce stove top to medium-low heat and add vegetables, potatoes, soup, and milk to the cooked chicken.

4. Simmer mixture and warm thoroughly for five minutes.

5. Unroll top pie crust on flat surface and use small cookie cutter(s) to create a design on the crust. This will also allow steam to escape and allows us to express our art creativity with seasonal designs and shapes. Add the cut-out pieces to the top of the pie crust to decorate. Don't forget to have fun!

6. Add hot pot pie filling to the bottom baked pie crust and cover mixture with the top (uncooked) pie crust. Brush one tablespoon of melted butter on the top pie crust.

7. Bake in oven for 12 minutes or until crust is golden brown and pie filling is bubbly.

8. Broil on high for two minutes to crisp edges, if desired.

About the Authors:

Adelaide Farms is in a farming, fishing, and forestry town.
We help conserve natural resources in the water and on the ground.

Living in a waterfront community is absolutely the best.
The Chesapeake Bay is our backyard treasure chest.

Everyone has chores. "This is not a hotel!" Old Man Haynie would say.
With the help of their mother, they learn work ethic the Haynie way.

With a heart to serve and experience to lead,
Adelaide loves helping children add, subtract, write, and read!

Our generation is different. They say we are a new breed.
Our American Dream is similar. We still want the mule and forty-acre deed!

Suzette Banks

My oldest daughter is Suzette.
She loves being athletic and tall.
She read 1,000 books before kindergarten started in the fall.
She wants to sell lemonade to buy the horses a new stable and stall.

Juliette Banks

My younger daughter is Juliette.
She is very creative and scribbled crayon on the wall.
She loves pink jewelry, colorful tutus, and buying boots at the mall.
She loves running and being outdoors. Wherever she goes, she carries a stuffed doll.

About the Author:

Roslyn Haynie Banks is an advocate for financial literacy, financial freedom, and fair income tax legislation. She is an accountant, author, and angel investor for entrepreneurs. She enjoys teaching workshops and coaching taxpayers on strategies to increase their net cash flow. As a federal income tax practitioner, she serves a diverse niche of clients, globally, including military service members, veterans, and their families.

Roslyn currently holds an Enrolled Agent (EA) license from the United States Department of the Treasury Internal Revenue Service (IRS). After the annual April 15th tax deadline, she spends countless hours in the summer engaged in continuing education courses on ethics and tax law updates. Becoming an Enrolled Agent or a Certified Public Accountant (CPA) to specialize in income taxation requires a lifelong commitment to learning and serving. She has realized these unique community helpers truly work to preserve the integrity of worldwide tax systems and the global economy.

While completing her degree in finance from The College of William and Mary, she spent one semester in Adelaide, South Australia, to gain an international vision of the global economy. While obtaining her Master of Accounting (MAcc) degree, she fell in love with the United States Internal Revenue Code. After her first tax season managing a retail tax office, she passed all three levels of the Enrolled Agent exam on the first try!

Roslyn was born and raised as a fifth-generation farmer on her family farm in the rural Northern Neck of Virginia. She will always have a special appreciation for land ownership—especially since she knows it is not a depreciable asset! During the global COVID-19 health and economic pandemic, she returned to her hometown to assist with the family farming operations. Roslyn, along with her two daughters, were gifted fifteen baby chickens from her father in April 2020.

For more information, visit www.Hayniebanks.com.

About the Illustrator:

Bonnie Lemaire began her career as a freelance illustrator with a promotional post card in 1989. She is a graduate of Ontario College of Art's Communication and Design program, specializing in medical illustration.

Her first position as artist-designer was with Ganz and Brothers Canada, designing figurines and teddy bears! It was a valuable experience, catapulting her into a successful freelance career. She has seen her work utilized in many different projects, including home décor, giftware, stickers, toy design, and children's books.

Bonnie's eternal optimism is the foundation of every drawing. Silly, quirky, comical and curious characters come alive and dance on her pages.

Bonnie works in her home studio located in a small hamlet in Northern Ontario, Canada, with her furry friend Crowquill the studio cat.

Books she has illustrated have won many awards including Foreword Clarion 5-Star-Seal, NIEAseal-2014-Winner, and NewPinnacleAward.

Bonnie's eccentric creations within fantastical stories have brought smiles to small faces and delight to her readers all over the world. She continues to enjoy her work, drawing and painting while listening to crime and mystery audio books, Studio Gibli soundtracks, and endless reruns of the original Star Trek.

To see more of her work, please check out www.bonniella.com.

40573432R00024